God's Word for God's Children
The First Marriage
by Olin Edward James

Copyright © 2015
First edition published 2015
All rights reserved. No part of this book may be reproduced, stored in a retrieval system, or transmitted in any form or by any means – electronic, mechanical, photocopying, recording, or otherwise, without written permission from the publisher.
Illustrator: Jess Wadland
Author Family Photo: Esther Abel
Editor: Sharon Spencer

Printed in the United States of America
www.lifesentencepublishing.com
LIFE SENTENCE Publishing books are available at discounted prices for ministries and other outreach. Find out more by contacting us at info@lspbooks.com
LIFE SENTENCE Publishing, and its logo are trademarks of LIFE SENTENCE Publishing, LLC
P.O. Box 652
Abbotsford, WI 54405
RELIGION / Christian Life / Family
Paperback ISBN: 978-1-62245-189-0
Ebook ISBN: 978-1-62245-190-6
10 9 8 7 6 5 4 3 2 1
This book is available wherever books are sold.

About the Author

The author, raised by Godly parents, is from a small Ohio town. He is married to his wonderful wife, Christy, and has two incredible daughters, Hannah Katherine and Gwenyth Irene (thus the KathIrene Kids). He has studied God's word in Ohio, New York, and Alberta, Canada, and desires that all would read and love the Scriptures, abide in Jesus, walk in the Spirit, and glorify God.

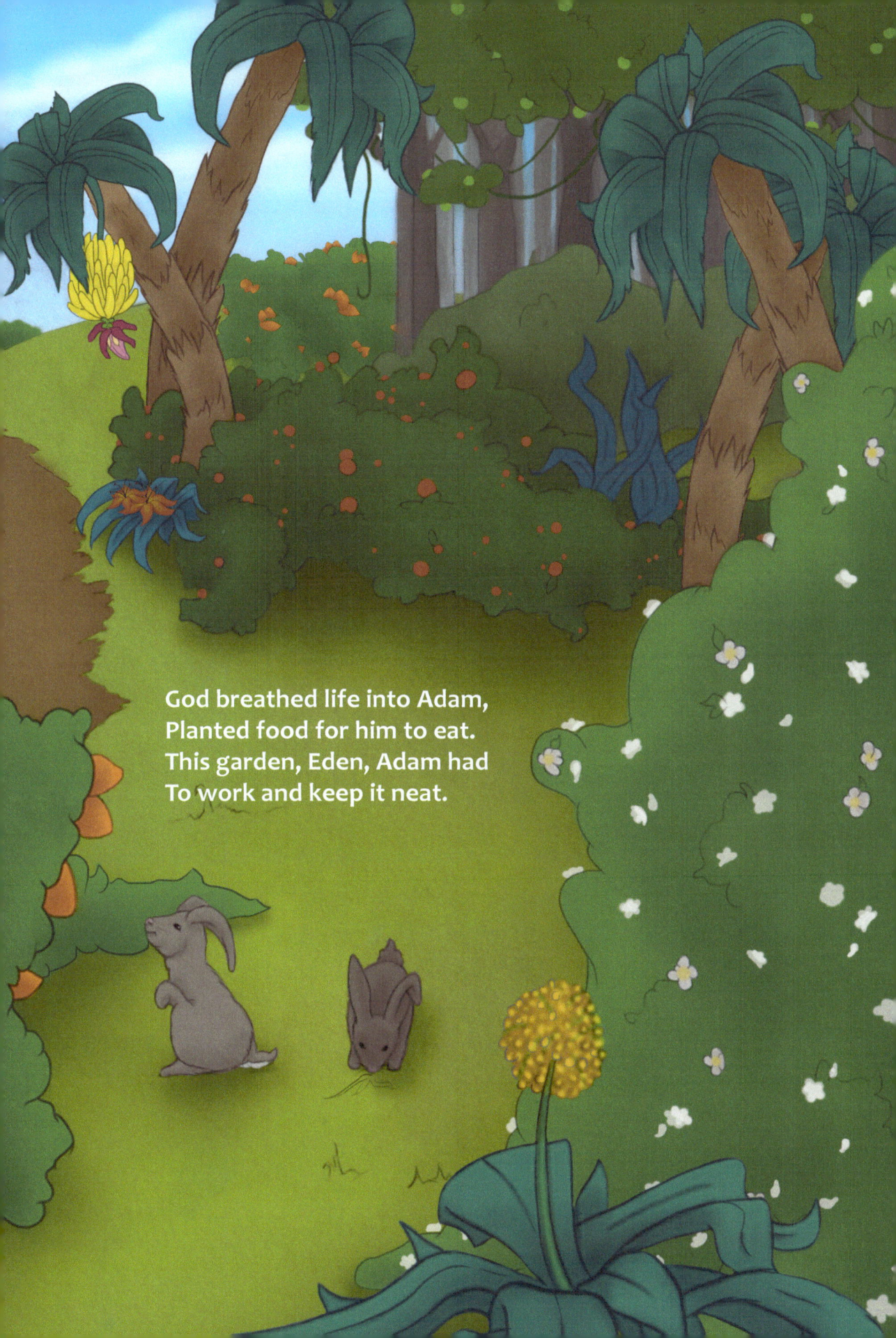

God breathed life into Adam,
Planted food for him to eat.
This garden, Eden, Adam had
To work and keep it neat.

God saw that Adam was alone—
No humans in his life.
He needed one to help him,
So God made for him a wife.

So God began our marriages—
A husband and a wife
Who love God and each other, and
Who stay that way for life.

www.ingramcontent.com/pod-product-compliance
Lightning Source LLC
Chambersburg PA
CBHW041123070526
44584CB00002B/265